Original title:
The Ficus Flow

Copyright © 2025 Creative Arts Management OÜ
All rights reserved.

Author: Adrian Caldwell
ISBN HARDBACK: 978-1-80566-702-5
ISBN PAPERBACK: 978-1-80566-987-6

Leaves Like Lush Lullabies

In the garden, greens conspire,
Whispers tickle, leaves on fire.
Swaying gently, what a tease,
Hiding secrets, dancing trees.

A squirrel slips, a tumble low,
Chasing shadows, putting on a show.
With acorn hats, they prance around,
In leafy laughter, joy is found.

Beneath the Maelstrom

Beneath the branches, chaos reigns,
A raccoon struts, with his gains.
Dodging raindrops, what a sight,
Caught in puddles, quite the fright!

A parrot caws a cheeky tune,
As frogs croak loudly, like a shoon.
Nature's frolic, wild and free,
Underneath the grand old tree.

Dappled Light's Embrace

Sunlight dances, pick a spot,
Playing hide and seek, quite forgot.
Frogs in hats, they meet and greet,
Discussing tales, oh so sweet.

A fluttering leaf, whispers low,
Says the jokes are quite a show.
While beetles bob and roll about,
Who knew nature could laugh out loud?

Dance of the Verdant Spirits

In a leafy ball, spirits sway,
Twisting, twirling, night and day.
A cheeky breeze joins the spree,
Tickling branches, oh so free.

With giggles hidden in the air,
They whisper secrets, a lively affair.
Mischievous vines in a tangle bind,
An uproar of joy, so unconfined.

Paths of Positivity

In a garden where the branches sway,
Bouncing leaves dance the day away.
A squirrel prances, feeling bold,
Telling secrets of stories untold.

With every twist, smiles collide,
Wiggly worms join the leafy ride.
Sprouts giggle as they poke through dirt,
Life's humor in every sprout and turt.

Leafy Legacies

Once a twig, now a tree so grand,
Whispers of laughter in every strand.
Branches stretch, and shadows play,
   Older leaves have much to say.

Naps under foliage, a cozy spot,
Shady giggles in the sun's hot spot.
Frogs offer riddles in soft croaks,
Nature's punchlines from barky folks.

Green Reflections

Mirrored leaves giggle at the sky,
Rehearsing jokes the birds pass by.
In this leafy world, jokes unfold,
Greenery's tales, both brave and bold.

Reflections shimmer in puddles bright,
Where even raindrops get a fright.
Chirpy notes fill the air with glee,
Nature's jesters, wild and free.

A Mosaic of Life

In a vibrant patchwork, life unfolds,
Stories come wrapped in green and gold.
Petals wink at the passing breeze,
Tickling laughter among the trees.

Bees buzz humor so sweet and light,
Polling jokes from morning till night.
Life a canvas of winks and grins,
With every leaf, a chuckle begins.

Under the Leafy Veil

Under a giant leaf, I find my hat,
A squirrel dashes by, what's up with that?
He points at my lunch, then starts to grin,
I laugh as he leans, trying to sneak in.

The sun peeks through, a meadow of light,
While ants practice cartwheels, what a sight!
The caterpillar's dance is a slow-motion spree,
With moves like a dance floor, wild and free.

Gentle Giants of the Grove

Tall and wise, the elders stand,
Branches wave like they're in a band.
A rabbit hops by, winks with a twitch,
While the tree whispers back, 'Life's a fun pitch!'

Birds chirp jokes, the leaves all shake,
As the breeze stitches laughter, no heart can break.
Nearby, a deer attempts a ballet,
But trips on a root—oh no! What a display!

The Embrace of Ecosystems

In the embrace of green, all friends convene,
A turtle's slow stroll makes for a scene.
While a frog on a lily pad croaks out loud,
His solo performance draws quite the crowd.

The flowers gossip with buzzing bees,
While the shadows chuckle in cool, gentle breeze.
Each creature plays a part—some sly, some sweet,
It's a comedy show on nature's own sheet.

Tranquil Treasures

Under the stillness, treasures align,
A beetle plays poker, feeling divine.
With twigs for chips and acorns for bets,
The stakes are high—though no one regrets.

A snail checks his watch, 'Time creeps ahead!'
While a grasshopper snaps, 'Life's merely a thread.'
In this tranquil realm, humor unfurls,
As nature's own jesters dance and twirl.

Lush Secrets Unraveled

In the garden where whispers dwell,
A plant with tales it dares to tell.
Squirrels giggle as they prance,
While roots wiggle in a lively dance.

Leaves are hats for the roaming gnomes,
Dancing shadows call it home.
A lizard slips with a tiny sneeze,
Underneath that leafy tease.

Swaying to the Rhythm

Beats of nature start to play,
Everything twirls in a funky way.
A funky breeze, the branches swing,
While insects hum and birds all sing.

Funky fruit drop, they make a mess,
As squirrels leave their nutty stress.
A babbling brook joins the jam,
Making sure there's plenty of spam.

Cradle of Tranquility

In a calm corner where laughter grows,
A cozy nook where no one knows.
Sunlight trickles through leaves so bright,
As giggles bounce in pure delight.

A sleepy cat sprawls on a branch,
Dreaming of fish, oh what a chance!
A butterfly did a silly spin,
While ants play tag with a silly grin.

Embracing the Wild

In the wild where craziness reigns,
Crazy critters drop their chains.
A raccoon sings a silly tune,
While the moon giggles, oh so soon.

Bouncing bunnies break dance at night,
Under stars that shine so bright.
Branches swing with a playful nudge,
As nature laughs, we won't judge.

Beneath the Canopy's Whisper

In a jungle of chatter, the leaves play a game,
Each rustle a secret, each bend a new name.
Squirrels hold meetings, on branches so wide,
Debating the merits of a nut-based ride.

Beneath the vast shade where shadows convene,
Laughter erupts from the branches, quite keen.
A parrot mimics the gossiping breeze,
While a sloth rolls his eyes, planning to tease.

Dreams Nestled in Green

In a world made of green, where the daylight can prance,
Lies a kingdom of dreams, eager for chance.
A worm in a tuxedo is throwing a ball,
Pasta made of leaves, served up in a hall.

The ants bring the rhythm, the beetles have style,
While spiders swing dances, their webs seen with guile.
Crickets play tunes with a tune of delight,
In this green little dream, they dance through the night.

The Hidden Stories of Roots

Roots are the legends, beneath earth they dwell,
Whispering tales that they'll never tell.
A potato claims fame for being the star,
While carrots just grumble, saying, 'We're bizarre!'

Worms start a ruckus, saying, 'Look who's in charge!'
But the mighty oak laughs, 'You're not even large!'
It's a party below, with roots intertwined,
Sharing the craziest stories they find.

Rhythms of Renewal

The wind plays a song, oh what joy it brings,
As leaves twirl around like they're wearing new bling.
A tree leaps with joy, in a quirky ballet,
While a squirrel scatters nuts in a wild cabaret.

Vines sway with laughter, their tendrils a dance,
Entwining all creatures that happen to prance.
Nature's own rhythm, it's pulsing with glee,
Life's a hilarious game, come play with me!

Threads of Verdant Memory

A green thread weaves through the air,
Leaves gossip secrets with flair.
Bugs hold a conference on what's fair,
While shadows twist and dance with care.

The roots are busy, plotting schemes,
To take over the garden, it seems!
A raccoon peeks in, lost in dreams,
While squirrels plot to steal all the creams.

Each branch tells tales of sunlit days,
As branches wiggle in playful ways.
Nature laughs at the sun's harsh rays,
And drips with joy when it rains and sways.

From nutty acorns, wisdom sprouts,
With twists and turns, nature shouts.
A tangled web of roots and doubts,
Where laughter echoes, leaving no droughts.

A Canopy of Connection

Under a canopy, oh what a sight,
Where birds hold meetings, taking flight.
The leaves high-five as squirrels hold tight,
While laughter echoes into the night.

A branch turned swing is fun and wild,
While nature's secrets are seldom mild.
An owl plays poker, oh what a child,
With branches as chips, he's terribly styled.

The vines tell stories, sometimes quite tall,
Of daring escapes, and some that stall.
A chuckle erupts when the branches fall,
Nature's giggles echo, a harmless brawl.

As sunlight dances, casting a game,
Each leaf a player, none are the same.
In this leafy realm, we all stake claim,
Where humor is woven, with roots to fame.

Nature's Quiet Conversations

Close your eyes, hear nature's chat,
Leaves chuckle softly, imagine that!
A snail just slipped, oh what of that?
As ants work together, chasing the fat.

Branches bend low to share a joke,
While beetles debate, and sunlight pokes.
A butterfly flutters, wearing a cloak,
With whispers so sweet, it gently strokes.

The mosses murmur, wise and slow,
This forest party's all in the know.
With every rustle, the laughter will grow,
As frogs croak punchlines all in a row.

A dance of shadows, a flutter of wings,
Nature's humor in the smallest of things.
Oh, how the laughter sweetly sings,
In a world where joy effortlessly clings.

Fertile Whispers

Roots ramble softly beneath the ground,
In the quiet, mischief is found.
Whispers of daisies, laughing around,
As insects tell tales with no one to hound.

Soil's murmurs are thick with delight,
As sunbeams tickle with playful light.
A worm tells a tale of a most fanciful flight,
While daisies giggle with all of their might.

The dew drops dance, in laughter they sway,
As little critters frolic in every way.
"Don't eat my leaves!" the plants might say,
But nature's jesters will not dismay.

In fertile laughter, this world spins round,
Every leaf and petal in joy is bound.
Echoing chuckles, sweet and profound,
In this wondrous garden, fun is found.

The Rise of Verdure

In a pot sat a plant, so stout and so proud,
With bravado it claimed, 'I'm the best in the crowd!'
It stretched to the sun, with leaves wide and bright,
Saying, 'Bask in my glory, I'm quite the sight!'

A squirrel stopped by, gave a wink and a nod,
'Such a leafy affair, did you pray to a god?'
'I don't need divine, just ample sunshine,'
Said the plant with a grin, 'I'm perfectly fine.'

Stories Unfurled in Green

Once a bud dared to speak, on a branch way up high,
'The wind has a tale, but I'll give it a try!'
With a twist and a turn, it started to sway,
'Let me tell you a story, in my leafy display!'

A caterpillar laughed, wiggling with glee,
'Your story needs action, a plot twist for me!'
'Fear not,' said the bud, 'I'll grow a surprise,
A flower will bloom, watch it dazzle your eyes!'

Hues of Harmony

In a garden so bright, colors danced all around,
'Pigments of joy,' they declared, 'can be found!'
A blue jay exclaimed, 'I'm the star of the show,
But green's not too shabby, I promise you so!'

Yellow blooms chuckled, sharing secrets of sun,
'We sparkle and shimmer; it's so much fun!'
While reds piped up, 'We'll paint the town bold,
With humor and warmth, our stories unfold!'

Forested Fantasies

In a grove where squirrels scheme,
Bouncing leaves chase each dream.
Trees gossip in the breeze,
Mushrooms dance with utmost ease.

Toadstools wearing tiny hats,
Whisper secrets with the bats.
Raccoons play a jazz refrain,
While chipmunks chuckle, loose and vain.

A chubby owl spinning tales,
Plotting pranks with fluttered gales.
Woodpeckers drum a lively beat,
While laughter echoes off the fleet.

The Quiet Chronicles

Silent branches make a fuss,
As crickets ride the garden bus.
The shadows giggle, twist, and twine,
While fireflies ink the stars' design.

Mossy carpets host a show,
As bunnies hop—oh, what a glow!
A fox in glasses reads a book,
While raccoons on the sidelines look.

A snail in sneakers sprints away,
In slow-motion—what a play!
A hedgehog plays the tambourine,
Beneath the moon, a vibrant scene.

Breath of the Bough

Branches stretch, a yoga class,
Leaves giggle, oh what a pass!
A caterpillar takes a leap,
As grasshoppers start to creep.

The sun pokes through with rays of cheer,
And ants perform the dance we cheer.
A toad croaks out a funny tune,
While shadows sway beneath the moon.

A chameleon, in socks so bright,
Nails the art of hide-and-sight.
Squirrels race with acorn snacks,
As laughter fills the forest tracks.

Enveloping Eden

In the shade of vibrant hues,
Lemons laugh, but not the blues.
While parrots paint the air with glee,
And frogs audition for a spree.

With vines draped in laughter's thread,
A worm spins tales from his bed.
The daisies wear their brightest grin,
While bees join in a buzzing din.

A couple of owls start a choir,
Singing tunes that never tire.
In this realm of joy and play,
Nature's joke just sways away.

Roots of Resilience

Beneath the soil, they wiggle and twine,
A party of roots, sipping sunshine fine.
They laugh and they dance, in the dark and the dirt,
"Let's grow a big tree!" they cheer, full of spurt.

With every new sprout that pops in a rush,
They tickle the worms, cause a ground-shaking hush.
"Catch me if you can!" the bravest would shout,
As the plants giggle softly, twirling about.

Sunlight's Tender Caress

Oh bright yellow beams, do you tickle my leaves?
I bask in your warmth like a cat on eaves.
"Hey there, dear Sun! Care for a game?"
I wiggle and jiggle, and it's never the same.

With a wink and a grin, I soak up your glow,
As photosynthesis turns me into a pro.
"I'm a veggie magician, watch this leafy trick!"
With a twist and a twirl, I'll grow really quick!

Shades of Serenity

Under my canopy, all worries will fade,
A cool little nook where the stress is allayed.
"Come snuggle with me!" I say to a bug,
He wiggles and laughs, feeling snug as a rug.

The breeze plays a tune, as leaves gently sway,
A jazz band of shadows, inviting to play.
"Let's chill here forever, just you and I,"
The insects all gather, beneath the sky.

In the Shade of Wisdom

Gather 'round, world, and listen to me,
I've seen lots of things from my perch on this tree.
"Life's a wild ride, with twists and with bends,
But just take a seat! Here, your journey transcends."

The squirrels share secrets, the birds sing with glee,
In whispers and giggles, from branches we see.
"And when it gets tough, just laugh a bit loud,
For humor's the sunshine that brightens the crowd!"

Dancing with the Vines

In a garden where laughter grows,
Vines twist and twirl like a circus show.
Branches sway to a whimsical tune,
While critters dance under the moon.

Every leaf has a joke to share,
Whispered secrets hang in the air.
A squirrel in a top hat takes his stand,
As giggles ripple through the land.

Lizards join in, dressed to impress,
Their dance moves, I must confess!
With each step, they bump and glide,
Nature's party can't be denied.

As night falls, the fun's not done,
The garden's a stage; it's all in good fun!
So grab a partner, don't delay,
Let's keep dancing till light of day!

Harmony in the Green

In the realm where green reigns supreme,
Leaves chime in with a bubbly theme.
A rabbit hops in rhythm, with glee,
While flowers giggle at the bumblebee.

Vines tickle the clouds above,
Swaying, whispering secrets of love.
The breeze plays tunes on the leaf's skin,
As squirrels tap dance, reveling in sin.

A toad croaks a melody bright,
Under the twinkling stars of night.
With wiggly worms as the backup crew,
Their wobbly moves make you smile, too!

Laughter echoes through the boughs,
Nature's laughter—all of us wow!
In harmony, let's sing along,
In this green kingdom where we belong.

The Language of Leaves

Leaves chatter like a giddy crowd,
Telling tales, oh-so-loud!
With rustles, they share the latest news,
Gossiping softly like they're on cruise.

Each flutter a pun, each twist a joke,
As sunlight paints the air with smoke.
The branches bow with merry cheer,
Inviting all creatures to gather near.

A woodpecker pecks with style and flair,
Tapping out beats that tickle the air.
Leaves laugh so hard, they start to shake,
Even the roots join in for a break!

With nature's orchestra all around,
Every chuckle an echo, deeply profound.
In this grove where the laughter weaves,
We converse in the joyous language of leaves!

Echoes of Nature's Heart

In a forest alive with cheer,
Echoes giggle from far and near.
The trees tease the wind with their grace,
Nature dons a bright, silly face.

A bear slips on a banana peel,
With a wobble and bounce, what a funny deal!
While owls hoot riddles in moonlit halls,
The shadows chuckle as the night falls.

Each rustling leaf has a jest to share,
While crickets chirp a foot-tapping flare.
The brook chuckles as it flows by,
Painting smiles under the wide-open sky.

As dawn breaks, with giggles still fresh,
Sunbeams dance, a playful mesh.
Echoes of joy in every part,
Nature's laughter—the beat of its heart!

Canopy Conversations

Beneath the leafy dome so wide,
Chatting squirrels take a ride.
Whispering winds in playful tones,
Tickling branches, making moans.

Breezy tales of acorn heists,
Raccoons plan their midnight feasts.
With every rustle, laughter rings,
Nature's jokes on little wings.

A chorus of chirps, so absurd,
Who knew a bush could say a word?
Mischief twirls in dappled light,
Making shadows dance at night.

In the tree, a wise old owl,
Mocks the crows with a knowing scowl.
With branches bowed, they groove and sway,
A leafy laugh keeps gloom at bay.

Verdant Visions

In every leaf, a tale unfolds,
Of stuck-up roots and dandelion gold.
The mossy carpet giggles with glee,
As ladybugs host a tea party spree.

Bouncing bunnies in a leafy race,
Trying hard to keep their pace.
The bushes giggle, "What a sight!
Who knew these critters could take flight?"

Underneath the bustling sun,
Playful shadows seem to run.
While vines tie knots, a dance ensues,
Tree trunks hum silly, ancient blues.

With nature's laughter echoing loud,
Each twig wears joy like a proud shroud.
In this green realm, carefree and spry,
The smallest things let laughter fly.

The Language of Leaves

Every leaf has secrets to share,
With gossip flowing through the air.
"Did you hear about the worm on a spree?
He thought he was a leaf—so free!"

Roots whisper jokes beneath the ground,
While snails take bets on who's the slowest around.
Branches sway with stories they weave,
Of easy lives, "Just believe!"

In the sun, misfit flowers bloom,
Competing for a spot, they're making room.
"Who's the showiest?" they pout and plead,
As bees roll their eyes, saying, "Succeed!"

With every rustle, a chuckle rings,
In this green realm, hilarity springs.
Leaves flutter down with a playful cheer,
Knowing tomorrow, more laughs will be near.

Infinite Green Horizons

A meadow sprawls with patches bright,
Where dandelions dance, a cheeky sight.
Grass blades poke and tease the toes,
Of wandering feet who spill their woes.

In the thickets, critters play along,
Singing silly tunes, they feel so strong.
With every jump, a thump and thud,
The leafy crowd bursts into bud.

Trees don hats made of pinecone caps,
While wandering squirrels hold epic maps.
"Let's find the craziest nut," they shout,
Creating a ruckus, hash and clout.

Infinite laughter spins through the air,
As flowers gossip without a care.
In this world of green delight,
Joyful chaos makes everything feel right.

Stories in Every Leaf

Once a leaf whispered a tale,
Of a squirrel who got lost in a pail.
It danced in the breeze, oh so free,
Mocking the cat who stared up a tree.

A hundred stories tangled on boughs,
Each one weaves a smile or a wow.
From the ants that throw wild tea parties,
To the mice that share cheesy smarties.

When rain drops fall, the leaves giggle,
As puddles form and the froggies wiggle.
A plot twist here and a punchline there,
In the cool shade, laughter fills the air.

The sun setting, the leaves reminisce,
About funny things they couldn't dismiss.
In every green inch, joy and delight,
Who knew eavesdropping could be so bright?

Tides of Tranquility

In a breeze so soft, it sways with glee,
Leaves wave like they're having a spree.
Branches stretch out for a quick high five,
As birds zoom past, feeling alive.

Sunset paints colors, orange and green,
Yet, the snails think it's quite the scene.
Slowly they travel on leafy trails,
With gossip plans over snail-sized pails.

A rabbit hops in, to share a joke,
About the fish who fancied to smoke.
The leaves chuckle, their giggles flow,
As nature's stage takes on a show.

With the moon above, the night's at play,
The trees giggle till the break of day.
For tranquility isn't just calm sleep,
But laughter that echoes, oh so deep!

Urban Oasis

In a city where cars zoom and clash,
One tiny sprout makes its green splash.
It stretches through concrete, a brave little dude,
Sipping coffee, feeling quite rude.

Beneath the hustle, a shaded retreat,
Where pigeons gather and gnaw on their treat.
A gathering spot for the quirky and odd,
With laughter and chat, the weird they applaud.

As a bus honks loud, they shush with a grin,
They whisper sweet secrets, as the chaos spins.
"Oh look," says a sprout, "there's a bear in the park!"
A couple of kids scream, "Where?! In the dark?"

The roots weave stories of wild urban dreams,
Amid tall buildings, they burst at the seams.
The oasis blooms where life's twists and turns,
And in every shout, an adventure returns!

A Tapestry of Roots

In the garden's embrace, roots intertwine,
Plotting a romp for the sun to shine.
"Hey fellow roots, what's the latest scoop?"
They giggle and shimmy, a deep underground troop.

They trade their stories in whispers so sweet,
Of a worm who danced to a funky beet.
And a snail who tried to leap like a frog,
Only to find he'd wedged in a log.

With each wiggle and bob on the ground,
They dance to the rhythm of nature's sound.
"Let's invite those weeds for a game of charades,"
And soon there's a riot in leafy parades.

Through the dirt, they weave a colorful tale,
Of laughter and joy in a life that won't pale.
For in every nudge of a root, there's a jest,
In the grand tapestry where funny thrives best!

Serene Interludes

In the garden where leaves confide,
A squirrel ran with a nut so wide.
It slipped and tumbled, what a sight,
Even the flowers laughed in delight.

Sunbeams dance on dew-kissed grass,
A frog leapt high, a leap of sass.
He landed headfirst, squished a snail,
But both just shrugged, they can't be frail.

With a breeze that tickles the trees,
A raccoon sneezes, if you please!
As petals flutter in merry cheer,
Nature's jokes are crystal clear.

Underneath the shade, they play,
Well, who needs work on a sunny day?
Laughter mingles with bees on a spree,
Life's a giggle in harmony.

The Gentle Breath of Nature

A breeze hiccupped, trees swayed anew,
A chubby chick turned and flew.
He missed his mark and hit the lawn,
Landed with fluff, 'I'm not a fawn!'

Clouds chuckled, sharing gossip so light,
As raindrops tumble, a silly sight.
One splashed a turtle, 'you're on my case!'
The turtle grinned, 'I found my place!'

Butterflies in their tutu's dance,
While ants march on, without a chance.
One lost its way and did a twirl,
'Is this a parade, or just a whirl?'

Birds snicker at their own duets,
Mistakes are fine, no regrets!
Nature's giggles make spirits rise,
Where laughter's the sweetest surprise.

Whispers Beneath the Bark

In groves where whispers twirl and spin,
A beetle claimed that he could win.
He raced a leaf on its autumn glide,
But oops! It flew; oh, what a ride!

The trees recount tales of love-up-high,
While mice hold court, oh my, oh my!
A tiny court jester, with a grand bow,
Makes all the brambles giggle now.

Twisting vines weave a web of fun,
Chasing shadows in the sun.
A crow caws loudly, trying to tease,
But swayed by the laughter, he lost with ease.

Under the roots, a party starts,
Mushrooms dance, stealing some hearts.
In this merry chaos of green and gold,
Nature's funny stories unfold.

The Art of Growing

Sprouts stretch high towards the light,
A worm wiggles, 'This feels right!'
Too much rain, a little drip,
And plants just giggle at a slip.

A garden gnome gave a wink,
As daisies nodded, what do you think?
'We've got potential, just look at us!'
'Or maybe just flowers to make a fuss!'

Tomatoes blush in shades so bright,
While peppers puff, pretending to fight.
A carrot toppled, 'Oh what a mess!'
The radishes chuckled, 'A little less stress!'

In this patch of playful cheer,
Every sprout has its own frontier.
So let's embrace this garden's glow,
With roots so silly, watch us grow!

Nature's Silent Symphony

In the garden, squirrels dance,
A leaf's pirouette, take a chance!
Birds chirp jokes in harmony,
Nature's laugh, a comedy.

Breezes tickle branches high,
Wiggling leaves say, 'Oh my, oh my!'
Even shadows play their part,
Tickling sunbeams, a work of art.

A worm hums tunes in the dirt,
While ants march on, all in a flurt,
Critters wear tiny hats of grass,
Throwing a party, let's all pass!

So join the fun, don't be shy,
Nature's giggles reach the sky.
With every rustle, joy's alive,
In this scene, we all thrive!

Life Within the Leaf

Nestled snug beneath the green,
Life's antics often go unseen.
Ladybugs play peek-a-boo,
While caterpillars munch their stew.

A grasshopper jokes, jumps in style,
"Why did the leaf smile? Just a while!"
With tiny legs and silly stunts,
In the foliage, they make their hunts.

Roots gossip deep, secrets share,
"Do you think the sun's too fair?"
And flowers giggle, "Not a care,
Let's scatter seeds, lift in the air!"

So here we sit, we laugh, we play,
Life within the leaf, hooray!
Every twist, a wondrous tale,
In nature's world, we shall not fail!

Whispers of Green Canopies

Up above where branches sway,
Whispers float, come out and play.
A crow cracks jokes, spreads them wide,
In this green world, we'll confide.

Swaying vines do the twist,
Each rustle feels like a jest missed.
"Did you hear about the tree?"
"Just branched out, now feels fancy!"

Squirrels hold a nutty chat,
Winking at the passing cat.
Leaves burst out in playful shouts,
"Join us, join us! No doubts!"

So let the canopies giggle bright,
In this leafy world, all feels right.
With every rustle, every tone,
Nature's whispers, a cozy home!

Roots in Rhapsody

Deep down where giggles grow,
Roots twist and turn, in steady flow.
"Did you hear the plant's big dream?"
"It wants to dance, or so it seems!"

With mighty hugs, roots intertwine,
"Let's have a party, feel divine!"
Vines snicker as they climb high,
"Look at us, we can touch the sky!"

Moss plays soft, a plushy rug,
While mushrooms laugh, give you a hug.
"Why did the sapling bring a hat?"
"Because it's trendy, just like that!"

So let the roots sing their refrain,
In rhapsody, let the joy remain.
Every twist, a laughter spree,
In verdant depths, wild and free!

Nature's Hidden Cadence

Beneath the leaves, a whisper sounds,
A dance of roots in undergrounds.
The squirrels chuckle, watching the scene,
As nature's rhythm plays so keen.

With branches swaying, a leafy jig,
A nutty fox joins in, oh so big.
The breeze joins softly, just for a laugh,
Creating a symphony on the path.

Each twig a wand, casting spells so bright,
Where shadows giggle under the light.
The grass tickles toes on the run,
In this playful world, we find our fun.

Amidst the green, a bounce in the air,
Flowers tease bees, unaware they stare.
Nature's comedy, full of delight,
In her hidden cadence, all feels right.

Tresses of Tranquility

Long strands of green, a soft embrace,
Crowned by blossoms, a colorful face.
Small creatures skitter, with giggles so true,
In this tranquil mane, they find something new.

The lizards dance upon the leaves,
Laughing at shadows, playing as thieves.
A breeze comes sweeping, teasing their hair,
It's a raucous party, without a care.

With every rustle, tales come alive,
Of faeries and mischief, where dreams thrive.
The sun peeks through, tickling the kiss,
Of nature's tresses, a moment of bliss.

In this lush wonder, where smiles blend,
The joy of the earth, no need to pretend.
Wrapped in green, we twirl with glee,
Finding our peace, in laughter's decree.

On the Edge of Green

Where grass meets sky, a line so fine,
In the dance of the breeze, all things align.
With birds in chorus, who could resist?
They croon about life with a quirky twist.

A daisy pokes fun at a passing snail,
Who dreams of speed, but it's destined to fail.
While ants march along with a proud little tune,
They never stop chatting, not even at noon.

Under the sun, the shadows play games,
Making silly faces, forgetting their names.
In laughter we spiral, a silly parade,
On the edge of green, all troubles do fade.

Each flick of a leaf, a wink and a grin,
Nature's humor wrapped softly within.
So come join the fun, where smiles are free,
On this lush frontier, just you and me.

Luminous Lattice of Life

Through tangled vines, a glow so bright,
Nature's canvas, a whimsical sight.
Leaves laugh and shimmer, as sunlight spills,
Painting the world with curious thrills.

With mushrooms that giggle and wisps of smoke,
They plot little pranks, with each playful poke.
The critters conspire, a grand masquerade,
In this vibrant lattice, the fun never fades.

A rabbit with sunglasses lounges at noon,
While crickets hold concerts, oh what a tune!
The world spins in laughter, a joyous refrain,
Where shadows and sunlight are best friends in vain.

Amidst this glow, where wonders collide,
Nature's own humor is hard to hide.
So bask in the light, let your spirits soar,
In a luminous lattice, forever explore.

Fragile Futures

In a pot so wide, here I've grown,
With leaves like jokes, they're well-known.
I sway to whispers and sing to the sun,
But oh, dear soil, don't run, don't run!

The neighbors stare, oh what a sight,
As I dance and twirl, day and night.
My roots are tangled, like gossip in town,
Yet my humor keeps me from feeling down.

Oh, how my stems stretch high above,
Reaching for laughter, that's my true love.
While others just grumble and moan in despair,
I flip off the clouds with style and flare!

Frilly leaves flutter like kids in a game,
They giggle and tease, and I feel the same.
So fragile my future, yet so full of fun,
In this botanical realm, let's all be one!

A Canopy of Solace

Under a leafy roof, I sit tight,
Where squirrels joke, and birds take flight.
With branches that tickle and shadows that play,
I find my refuge from the day!

The sun sneaks in with a mischievous glance,
I laugh with the breeze, it's a merry dance.
The world below, so wild and loud,
But up in my haven, I'm super proud!

With nature's canvas, I chuckle and sigh,
Each leaf a meme, oh my, oh my!
A shade so silly, it lifts up my mood,
In this leafy laughter, I'm happily glued.

So come join my refuge, let's giggle away,
Amongst the vines and those who sway.
In this canopy of solace, let's have some fun,
A turtle, a bunny, all under one sun!

The Beauty Within Green

Oh, the beauty I find in shades of delight,
Green and lush, so vibrantly bright.
A funny paradox, I cling on and sway,
While pollen tickles and makes me go 'hay!'

The world sees beauty, I see a jest,
An artful disaster, a leafy quest.
Who knew that my leaves could draw such a crowd?
In laughter and joy, I wear it so proud!

Embracing my quirks with colors so bold,
A jester's garden where stories unfold.
With a wink from the earth, as I stretch and I grow,
Each part holds laughter, just thought you should know!

A beauty within that winks in disguise,
In every green layer, a giggle lies.
So toss me a smile, or a cheeky grin,
Finding beauty within all that's green!

Harmonies of the Jungle

In this jungle of chatter, where laughter is loud,
I sway to the rhythm, so happy and proud.
Gleeful, I flourish, a chorus of play,
With vines as my friends, we boogie all day!

With monkeys that tease and birds that croon,
Every rustle's a joke, and I'm feeling in tune.
A symphony of giggles floats high in the air,
In this lush little club, there's joy everywhere!

From roots to the tip, each branch is alive,
In this jungle's embrace, oh how we thrive!
So barrel through puddles, dance through the muck,
With drumming of raindrops, good fortune and luck!

Join me in laughter, as we swing side to side,
In this jungly ball, let's all take a ride.
Harmonies echo, that twinkle and sway,
While nature sings along to our playful ballet!

Dancing Light and Leaf

In the forest, leaves can prance,
With sunbeams joining in their dance.
They shimmy and shake without a care,
Whispering secrets to the air.

Squirrels chuckle, watching the show,
As twigs and branches start to glow.
A waltz of shadows and bright delight,
Wiggling under the moonlight.

The bugs are buzzing, trying to jive,
Grooving to rhythms, feeling alive.
Nature's party, wild and free,
Join the laugh, come swing with me!

Oh, the joy amongst green and brown,
Where even the roots wear a silly crown.
With every rustle, let laughter unfurl,
In a world where silliness swirls.

Sanctuary of the Sprouts

In a nook where small things grow,
Tiny sprouts put on a show.
With giggles and wiggles, they find their place,
A comedy act in nature's embrace.

Poking heads out from the earth's warm bed,
They tell jokes about leaves overhead.
"Why did the seed cross the ground?"
To prove it wasn't 'popping' around!

A haven for cheer, with roots so bold,
They dream of adventures, bright and gold.
Each little sprout, a clown in green,
Creating laughter in this leafy scene.

The buzzing bees join in the fun,
Tickling petals, on the run.
With each bloom, a chuckle ignites,
In this sanctuary of sprightly sights.

Cradled by Nature

Nestled snug, the flowers tease,
While the herbs waggle in the breeze.
Cradled in earth, warmth all around,
Where giggling critters abound.

Bunnies bounce and dance about,
Splashing joy, there's never doubt.
Nature's womb, a cozy spree,
Where even the rocks seem to agree.

Butterflies in their vibrant hues,
Whispering secrets, sharing clues.
Caught up in the fun, a wild parade,
In this cradle, nonsense is made.

The trees chuckle, swaying tall,
Showering laughter, love, and all.
With each bloom and rustle, feel the light,
In this gentle cradle, hearts take flight.

The Fine Line Between

In the garden, a balance so funny,
Where laughter meets the sweet honey.
A line drawn 'twixt giggle and glee,
As ants join in, full of esprit.

Blossoms tease with their bright colors,
While tiny critters scrape and hover.
"What's the deal with this fine line here?"
Nature grins, "It's crystal clear!"

From roots in chaos to petals in play,
Life weaves joy in a silly array.
Dancing on edges, the whimsy remains,
Spinning tales in nature's domains.

So come find the fun, in corners unseen,
Where laughter blooms, and joy reigns supreme.
A wobbly balance, like cats on a fence,
In every moment, life makes sense.

Shadows of Serenity

In a leafy world, so green and bright,
A tree named Fred danced with delight.
He wobbled and jiggled in the sun,
While squirrels giggled, oh what fun!

The branches waved, a comedic show,
With shadows that pirouetted below.
A leaf fell down like a clumsy mate,
And landed on a snail—what a fate!

A breeze blew through, tickling the air,
While bees buzzed around without a care.
Fred chuckled gently, his laughter contagious,
In the world of green, nothing was outrageous!

So here's to the giggles, the joy, the cheer,
In a shady haven that draws us near.
With every rustle, a new jest to find,
Nature's comedy, hilariously entwined!

The Pulse of the Plant

With roots in the ground, and a heart of soil,
A plant named Gladys loved to recoil.
Each time she heard a joke from a bee,
She'd wiggle and jiggle, so carefree!

Her leaves would flutter like hands in glee,
Whenever a critter told her a spree.
And when it rained, she'd wear a hat,
Made of playful puddles—imagine that!

The sunlight tickled her by the hour,
As she swayed and laughed, full of power.
With each golden beam, she felt alive,
In this wild garden, she would thrive!

So join in the fun, with Gladys around,
Where joy and laughter are always found.
In the pulse of the plant, there's a beat,
That dances and hops—oh, what a treat!

Symbiotic Secrets

In the tangled vines where mischief grows,
Lived critters who shared their silly prose.
A slug and a lizard, best friends in crime,
They plotted and giggled, oh what a time!

With whispers and chuckles among the leaves,
They'd fashion a throne made of twigs and tease.
A ladybug joined with a small little cheer,
Throwing a party that drew all near!

But a blast from the wind swept the snacks away,
And suddenly, chaos—oh, what dismay!
The slug slipped and slid, the lizard took flight,
In nature's great comedy, oh what a sight!

Yet through all the laughter, a truth they found,
In sharing a meal, their bond was profound.
So here's to the secrets all organisms share,
In life's garden theater, there's joy everywhere!

Enchanted Greenery

In enchanted woods lush with green,
Lived a plant who swore it was a queen.
With vines that curled, and leaves that twirled,
She ruled the garden, her laughter unfurled!

A rabbit in bowtie would hop by her side,
Sipping on nectar, full of pride.
While birds overhead sang catchy tunes,
And danced with the stars and the silvery moons!

As the flowers giggled in colors so bright,
The charm of the vines brought pure delight.
From dandelion wishes to the buzzing bee,
Each moment was magic—so carefree!

In this vibrant realm where joy took flight,
Laughter echoed wildly, both day and night.
With each little quirk of nature's delight,
Enchanted greenery glimmers so bright!

Echoes of the Earth

A leafy tree with a quirky grin,
Whispers secrets, lets the giggles in.
Roots like fingers tickle the ground,
As the wind plays hide and seek all around.

Beneath its shade, squirrels dance and leap,
Juggling acorns, oh what a heap!
A chorus of chirps joins the show,
Even the bugs put on a glow.

Mossy carpets, soft as a pillow,
Invites all creatures, every tiny fellow.
Giggles echo as branches sway,
Nature's humor in every play.

With each rustle and each creak,
Laughter rings where the branches speak.
The earth's a stage, come and see,
In this green world, wild and free!

Timeworn Tales of Nature

Once stood a tree, with tales to tell,
Of acorn ballads and root-bound spells.
A trunk with wisdom, wrinkled and grand,
Sharing its stories across the land.

Birds sit perched, wearing tiny hats,
Squawking lyrics, dressed as chitchats.
The beetles march like they own the way,
Waltzing together in a bug ballet.

Old branches groan in a comical fashion,
As the breeze tickles them into passion.
Leaves giggle as they twirl and glide,
In this whimsical world, there's no need to hide.

The roots gossip, tangled in fun,
A friendship made under the sun.
With the bark's chuckle and the sap's sweet tease,
Nature's humor is sure to please!

Serenity in Sap

A drop of syrup drips from the tree,
Sticky and sweet, quite a sight to see.
Creatures gather for the sugary taste,
In this moment, there's no time to waste.

A ladybug slides down with delight,
Claiming it's her special night.
The ants parade, a tiny troop,
At the sap feast, they happily scoop.

Laughter bursts as the wind starts to blow,
Tickling the leaves, making them glow.
A flutter of wings, a giggle or two,
Nature's jokes drifting softly through.

Sunlight dances on sticky treats,
Creating a mood that's hard to beat.
In the syrupy laughter that's sure to wrap,
Life flows sweetly from nature's sap.

Currents of Calm

A tranquil breeze fluffs up the leaves,
Whispers of nature, how it weaves.
Laughter bubbles like a brook nearby,
Nature's giggles dancing in the sky.

The shadows mingle, play hide and seek,
With lighthearted spirits that tickle the cheek.
A squirrel pauses, strikes a comical pose,
As if the world's a stage where it knows.

Clouds drift lazily, with fluffy grins,
Sharing jokes with the air and the winds.
Splashing colors, the sun winks and sways,
In this world of laughter, all fears decays.

Nature hums a silly tune,
With every rhythm, the flowers bloom.
In currents of calm, where smiles expand,
Join in the fun on this merry land!

In the Arms of Arbor

Under green branches, we giggle and sway,
Squirrels chuckle loudly, they dance all day.
A tree's slow embrace, a tickle or two,
Leaves rustling softly, like laughter anew.

Birds in a chorus, they sing out their tune,
While bees buzz around, they join in the fun.
As shadows grow longer, we lay on the grass,
With roots down below, just patiently pass.

Each branch like a hand, so gentle and wide,
Catching all our secrets, in laughter, we hide.
A trunk as our fortress, where stories unfold,
In this leafy palace, we're never too old.

So come take a seat, let's share a good pun,
In the shade of the leaves, our days are all won.
The world's spinning round, but here we stand still,
With nature's own humor, it's always a thrill.

Nature's Soft Serenade

Under the big boughs, a symphony plays,
With rustling leaves, it pulls us in sways.
The wind weaves through branches, a playful embrace,
Nature's own laughter, we join in the race.

A chorus of crickets, in night's velvet hue,
With a twist of their wings, they jiggle and coo.
The frogs join the party, with jumps and great leaps,
Making us chuckle, as nighttime slips deep.

Delighted by moonlight, the shadows take flight,
Trees mime our laughter, keen to join the night.
The soft underground thump, as roots tap in time,
Nature composed, with rhythm and rhyme.

So let's sway with the branches, arms open wide,
Join in this rhapsody, let giggles decide.
With leaves as our audience, they jeer and they cheer,
In nature's soft symphony, we lose all our fear.

Veins of Vitality

In leafy corridors, where life's pulse beats loud,
Nature's antics dance, as we giggle unbowed.
Vines twist and twirl, like a playful old friend,
With energy flowing, it never will end.

Roots wriggling jests, underground snickers abound,
While the trees poke their heads, peeking out all around.
A funny old owl with a wink and a sway,
At night he hoots jokes, in his wise, feathery way.

The rustle of leaves brings a chuckle or two,
As breezes conspire, with mischief anew.
Sap flows like laughter, warm through the vein,
Reminding us all, that joy isn't plain.

So gather round where the life force ignites,
Beneath playful canopies, full of delights.
With giggles and wiggles, let joy intertwine,
In this vibrant world, where life's veins brightly shine.

Groves of Gentle Dreams

In realms of green whispers, where giggles reside,
The trees tell tall tales, with branches as guides.
A blanket of blossoms, so fluffy, so light,
Cocooning our fancies deep into the night.

With faeries on leaves, and dreams of delight,
They tangle in roots under soft silver light.
Petals scatter laughter, like confetti on air,
Each moment a treasure, beyond earthly care.

Shadows of whimsy, play tag with the sun,
As the brook answers back, with a splashing fun run.
In this grove of giggles, illusions take flight,
While laughter flows freely, like stars in the night.

So dance through the thickets, let joy be your guide,
In this magical space, where our silliness hides.
With each gentle breeze, let your worries unspool,
In groves of sweet dreams, feeling blissfully cool.

Whispers of Leaves

In the garden, whispers rise,
Leaves discuss the clever flies.
"Did you see the cat today?"
"He thought he'd pounce, but slipped away!"

Squirrels play with acorn hats,
While birds plot to steal their snacks.
"That's my muffin!" one bird squawks,
As nutty thieves on tightropes walk.

Lizards sunbathe, striking poses,
Pretending to be garden roses.
"Look at me!" one impudently brags,
While trying hard to snag some rags.

The whispers grow, a leafy song,
Nature's humor, where we belong.
Join the chatter, it's quite a show,
In our little world where laughter grows.

Branches in the Breeze

Branches wiggle, they have fun,
Making shadows, oh so pun!
"Look at me!" a branch does shout,
"I'm the longest one about!"

A gust of wind, oops! They sway,
"Who needs a dance floor anyway?"
With every twist, a giggle shared,
As twigs and leaves declare they're spared.

In the breeze, they waltz and twist,
"I'm a dancer!" one insists.
"More like a flailer," another grins,
While insects cheer for playful spins.

Amidst the fun, a mockingbird,
Sings out jokes, got them all stirred.
Branch and leaf, they laugh so loud,
Nature's jesters, proud and unbowed.

Green Dreams Entwined

In the realm of vines and tours,
Plants tell tales of silly stours.
"Did you hear?" a petal cried,
"The cucumber tried to hide!"

He rolled away but got caught fast,
With little beans, they laughed and passed.
"I'm a fruit!" the hapless gourd quipped,
But laughter came as he just tipped.

Windy days bring fuzzy jokes,
As squash and peas share silly pokes.
"Why did the lettuce cross the path?"
"To get to the other salad, ha ha!"

In the garden of tangled delight,
Every leaf has a laugh tonight.
With whispers of joy that twirl and bind,
Green dreams are woven, hilariously intertwined.

Beneath the Canopy's Grace

Under the leafy shade they meet,
Banter of insects, quite a feat.
"Who's the funniest?" one barked loud,
Filling the air with a giggling crowd.

A caterpillar in a bow tie,
Said, "I'm chic! Just watch me fly!"
But alas, still stuck to a branch,
They love to tease and jest at chance.

A wise old tree just shakes its bark,
"Humor here is quite the spark!"
With laughter echoing through the wood,
In this green kingdom, all is good.

So join the fun, and laugh out loud,
Nature's jesters make us proud.
Beneath the canopy, life's embrace,
Laughter ripples in leafy grace.

A Symphony of Leaves

In a grove where shadows dance,
Leaves declare their leafy romance.
Branches sway to the wind's soft song,
Creating a rhythm where all belong.

A squirrel taps its tiny feet,
Joining in with a silly beat.
The sun winks through a leafy screen,
As nature jives, so fresh and green.

A gathering of bumblebees,
Happily buzzing amidst the trees.
They hum a tune that's quite absurd,
In harmony with the playful bird.

Laughter rustles through the boughs,
As breezes tickle the forest vows.
With every twist, the woodlands cheer,
In this symphony we hold so dear.

Secrets of the Shade

In the shade where secrets hide,
A chubby raccoon takes a ride.
Wearing shades, oh what a sight,
He thinks he's cool, but that's just fright!

Ants parade in their little line,
Marching like soldiers, so divine.
But tripping up on a fallen leaf,
They tumble down—what a comic grief!

A grumpy toad croaks from his throne,
Grumbling about being all alone.
Yet frogs leap in with cheerful croaks,
In their laughter, he just pokes jokes.

Underneath the leafy dome,
Creatures gather, make their home.
They share quirks, and witty lines,
In the shade, where humor shines.

Echoes in the Evergreen

Amidst the green, a giggle spins,
Where laughter echoes, joy begins.
A hedgehog tells tales of his plight,
As trees listen in pure delight.

A parrot mimics every sound,
His jokes are flying 'round and 'round.
He calls the owls his biggest fans,
Yet they just snooze in their tree branches.

Down by the brook, fish make a splash,
With silver scales that brightly flash.
They jump in sync, a fishy ballet,
Wowing frogs who cheer along the way.

With whispers soft and ticklish breeze,
Nature chuckles amidst the leaves.
In the green where laughter sings,
Echoes of joy, the forest brings.

Tendrils of Time

Vines unravel with silly flair,
Tugging at branches without a care.
They twist and twirl, a wild dance,
Thinking they've got all the chance!

A snail with swagger glides on by,
Wearing a shell that makes him fly.
He claims it's speed, but we all know,
He's just the slowest in the show!

Moss creeps in like a fuzzy rug,
While fungi sport a cheerful shrug.
They laugh at clocks that tick and tock,
Saying, 'In nature, time's just talk!'

Giggling roots join hands and sway,
In the party of plants, they love to play.
With each tickle from the passing breeze,
Tendrils of laughter dance through the trees.

Requiem in Green

In the garden of mischief, leaves sway,
A squirrel's acrobatics steal the day.
A dance-off with shadows, in sunlight's beam,
Nature giggles softly, a whimsical dream.

Underneath the branches, a secret plot,
The plants conspire, oh, what a lot!
To swap their potting soil for custard pie,
To tickle each root, oh my, oh my!

The flowers play charades, in bright attire,
Waving with petals, a giggly choir.
Bees start a conga, buzzing a tune,
While leaves throw a party beneath the moon.

So here's to the green, with smiles so wide,
Where every plant has too much green pride.
With laughter and joy, they'll never be seen,
Oh, what a show in this requiem green.

Tangles of Time

A vine creeps slowly, with jokes to tell,
Wrapping around secrets, oh, how they gel!
Time's a tangled yarn, a playful string,
Where laughter takes root, and the echo swings.

Branches sway like dancers, without a care,
Spreading leaves out, as if to declare:
"Don't rush through seasons, enjoy the climb,
Every twist and turn is a nursery rhyme!"

In this maze of green, confusion reigns,
Roots chuckle loud, teasing their chains.
How many leaves does it take to hide?
The neighbors peek over, their eyes open wide!

So let's spin and twirl in nature's own weave,
A tapestry tangled, it's hard to believe.
In laughter and whimsy, we'll savor the climb,
As we dance through the garden, lost in a rhyme.

Nature's Healing Hands

The sun sprinkles laughter on leaves so bright,
Turns the shy blooms into a colorful sight.
A dandelion thinks it can make us sneeze,
But it just tickles; nature's sense of tease!

The bushes whisper secrets, a comedic play,
While hedgehogs hide out, in clumsy ballet.
A mockingbird sings, with a voice quite bizarre,
As the trees shake their branches, a natural star!

Grass offers a cushion, to sit and unwind,
Inviting all critters of every kind.
With winks from the flowers, let's frolic and roam,
In nature's embrace, we find our true home.

So join in the laughter, let worries depart,
With each breeze that blows, mend every heart.
In this green sanctuary where humor expands,
We thrive under care from nature's own hands.

Where Green Hearts Beat

In a world of bubblegum and lively cheer,
Where trees share laughter, and vines draw near.
The roots giggle softly, a chuckle in earth,
As flowers debate their color and worth.

Where petals are painted with the hues of fun,
And grass serves lemonade under the sun.
A critter parade, all marching in tune,
As the moon giggles softly, 'til the thorns swoon.

Silly squirrels shuffle, a dance all their own,
While lizards throw shade on their little throne.
Here, green hearts beat to the rhythm of play,
With whispers of joy that never decay.

So grab a twig, let's dance in the light,
Where humor grows tall, as day turns to night.
Together we'll frolic, beneath leafy spires,
In a land where green hearts spark laughter's fires.

www.ingramcontent.com/pod-product-compliance
Lightning Source LLC
Chambersburg PA
CBHW051633160426
43209CB00004B/627